OF BREAKING GLASS
―――――――――――
Byrne

© 2022 James Byrne. All rights reserved; no part of this book may be reproduced by any means without the publisher's permission.

ISBN: 978-1-915079-97-8

The author has asserted their right to be identified as the author of this Work in accordance with the Copyright, Designs and Patents Act 1988

Cover designed by Aaron Kent

Edited and typeset by Aaron Kent

Broken Sleep Books Ltd
Rhydwen,
Talgarreg,
SA44 4HB
Wales

Contents

Burying the sound of breaking glass: an Introduction	9
5am. A candle named PROTECTION	13
First thing you remember	15
'R'	16
Death as contradictory gossip	17
Jukebox playlist	18
Sidewinder	20
Take off your skin	21
6am slowfire	22
Violence meaning passage	24
Under the rhyolite dome of Red Hill	26
To meet you here / I cannot	27
Enough antsypants	29
Wadjet	30
But there are no pythons in Death	31
In the parenthesis of fourteen months	32
The 'O' in sound gone quiet	33
Every dimple / a grain of sand	34
bridge vertigo's / highways / overpasses	36
Inventory	37
Memory un- / memory	38
Smear the triglycerides in	39
Inventory	40
Labyrinth you	42
Foucault tripped out under feast stars	43
Medicine bag like a lung	45
Alphabet of Losses	46

To think of you at your lowest point	47
We aren't golfers	49
The man in the Shoshoni office	50
Silence as vertebrae on Funeral Mountain	51
All this / towards this	52
Badwater, Shamanic initiation ritual	54
— Tunnel entrance to an old grotto	
— You looked at me from the flood marker	
— Sage smudge left wrist	
— Tunnel meaning: way in / way out	
— Brother, you never asked to come here	
— Trona sand / Badwater salt	
— Radiant the boy buying daffodils for his mum	
Black tomentum, sing	64
Two full moons hung over you	65
The Republicans	66
The Shoshoni elder	67
At the bar, three American jocks	68
Zabriskie Point	69
Antonioni fucking in the mule pass.	72
Eat up	74
Lumix precarious	75
Ballarat, Ghost Village	77
— A dirt path levels out to ask	
— Skeleton: did you come this way?	
— BloodBrother	
— art-i-fice!	
— A razor cuts the hand	
Zabriskie Point coda	84
Notes / Acknowledgements	87

Of Breaking Glass

James Byrne

for Robin
1973-2020

Sand from rock,
quartz into silica.

Burying the sound of breaking glass: an Introduction

During an extended trip to California earlier this year, it was difficult to grieve for my older brother who died unexpectedly the year before. Robin, who was severely agoraphobic, died alone in his room at the height of the initial Covid 19 lockdown in England. Though it's still possible Covid may have been involved, what we know is that he had suffered a major heart attack. He was 46 years old.

How could I connect with my brother's life out here, thousands of miles away from London, the city of his death? On the anniversary of his passing, I wrote Robin two letters and (intentionally) burned them to ash near Santa Monica pier. My brother wanted to be famous and would have loved the Americana glitz of Hollywood. I wrote a few poems for him along the Walk of Fame and published them privately among the family. I thought of my brother every day (still do) but, ultimately, I felt disconnected from being able to mourn his death—my connection to him being strongest in England. Towards the end of the trip, I realised I needed to escape the city and go somewhere relatively off-the-grid. Not really knowing what I would encounter there, I was drawn to visit the vast, echoing spaciousness of Death Valley.

A few years before he died, I asked Robin what was his first memory of being in the world. He replied that he wasn't sure: it was either a visual memory, or the memory of a sound. He was kicking in glass panels of a door whilst my mother and father argued in the bedroom upstairs. I suggested that perhaps his first actual memory was the sound of that same glass breaking and he agreed that the sonic would have preceded the visual.

Despite how my brother's mental health suffered throughout his adulthood, I am quite sure the formative experience of hearing glass break (he would have been 4 or 5 years old) must have damaged him profoundly. I wonder if he heard that sound (or echoes of it) throughout his life. When Robin first realised he couldn't live outdoors anymore, he was underground at Angel Islington tube station. He thought he was going to jump in front of a train as it screeched through a tunnel and onto the platform. Was this related to the sound of glass breaking too? A post-traumatic memory loop across time? Perhaps my brother never really had a chance to live beyond this initial trauma and tolerated it longer than anyone might reasonably expect during his short life.

The text that follows is a written record of my attempt to visit Death Valley to bury the sound of glass breaking.[1] For the three day trip, I bought a camera and would set it up at dawn, sometimes taking photographs (as included here) or filming. Occasionally I would perform rituals, such as the burning of sage and these involved a rendering of shamanic texts. One such ritual was an attempt to journey to 'the otherworld' and 'meet' my brother. I was to call upon a spirit animal (desert fox) and made use of an inventory of paraphernalia collected along the way in a medicine bag, smoking the contents out a stone jar in 'Badwater' (the lowest point in the U.S. and in the western hemisphere). I had never done anything like this before and the text from the rituals are recreated later in this book. They will form part of a short film to be premiered in London next year.

When I visited Death Valley it was June, during a major heatwave, a summer in which records were broken. Temperatures rarely dipped below 100º Fahrenheit whilst I was in the desert. I generally kept to the main tourist areas in the North East side of the valley: Artist's Palette, Badwater, Dante's View and Zabriskie Point. However, I also went along the road past Funeral Mountains towards the Armagosa Valley and past the state line into Nevada.

On my final morning, it had climbed up to 116º Fahrenheit and I still hadn't found a way to bury the sound of breaking glass. With a small urn full of sand, I drove out along an unmarked road to a final location, a ghost town called Ballarat. It was so hot there, I did not use my camera there for fear of it melting.

Though I kept my notebook open throughout mornings, because of the heat I often wrote up my thoughts later in the day at Furnace Creek, the lodge where I was based. At night I would self-medicate, either at the bar or in my room, trying to blot out the painfulness of the whole experience. One distraction was to watch *Zabriskie Point* by Michelangelo Antonioni, a film partly set in Death Valley, and write through the opening hour. I also chose to respond in the form of a coda to the Eisensteinian explosions in the film's final scene, whilst thinking of my brother, the disarray of his final possessions, as well as the pain he carried and various elements within the life he lived.

One of these possessions my brother left for me was the Egyptian snake goddess, Wadjet. This was from the time when Robin and I sold 'World Artefacts' on Camden Market, at the end of the 1990s, before his ambitious, globe-trotting business failed.

---

[1] Returning from Death Valley, I realised how the Trona area beyond Ridgecrest and to the east of Death Valley was, for many years, a major area of soda ash production, used to make various materials, including glass.

Coincidentally, on the night I received Wadjet, goddess of fertility, my daughter was conceived. Perhaps the anti-logic of grief led me to think of this as some kind of communication from Robin (a blessing if you like) beyond the grave. If I could connect with him somehow in the California desert, maybe he could show me how to me bury the sound that tormented him? More likely I would have to find a way to do this without and for him and for myself too (after all, I too was in the room when the glass of our childhood was being broken—sometimes I think I remember the sound being made).

In Death Valley, I went looking for my brother and found him everywhere (but also nowhere). Antonioni spoke about the nowhereness of Death Valley and how, for him, it was full of contradiction. With all its beauty and desolation, its violence and tranquillity, its explosive echoes and silences, I wonder how Death Valley might relate to the fragility of our own existence. The experience was a transformative journey through my brother's life and my ongoing processing of his death.

— August 31st, 2021

A Robin Red breast in a Cage
— William Blake

Look closer—his skin is a desert.
— Natalie Diaz

…the closer threat of life behind the glass.
— Jayanta Mahapatra

…la llaga melancólica de los adioses.
…the melancholy stigmata of goodbyes.
— Jaime Saenz

                                                                                                                 <Ridgecrest, Best Western>

5am. A candle named   PROTECTION lights the mirror darkness
of the street—

                Springer to the South
                Las Flores to the North
                        where last night
                                  you chowed down
              enchiladas verdes outside Olvera's.

                                              [What did you do?

                                  It was not enough]

Brother, in this light,
seeing / unseeing you

broken   yet half-
                                  recognisable

            as
            death
            is.

                                The wick fizzes
                                      grows dark—

                                                Just close the door and go.

First thing you remember—

    kicking in panels of glass
        as mum and dad
warred
    upstairs.

          It was the day
              he tried to strangle me.

          It was the night
              she came at me with a carving knife.

Brother,   how to bury the sound of breaking glass?

        [………………………………………]

If I could wash the blood from your feet.

          The tears that
                  tear.

'R'   *Ahhh*
   —ROBIN—

                    'R'   for 'Robbed'.

                         Ahh echoes night's chorus.

                                  The 'in'
                                         suffix

                            song   -   sheathed

                                    echoing
                            out

                                              (´   ´)

Everything
             caught up with you—
                           the no,
                                  the not yet.

Grief in the absence
                 of concrete nouns—

                                 Sk(in)

                                 (Ai)r

                                 Br(other)

Death as contradictory gossip

. . . .

                      What was that?

. . . .

Sometimes I carry the portrait of your face
like carrying an empty wallet   (´   `)

                    All this. And this

                                      [...................]

                                  like trying
                                            to assemble

                                  the lineage of ashes.

<Jukebox playlist, Spotify:
Ridgecrest - Death Valley National Park>

Primal Scream, 'Loaded': White chalklines. Wildrose peaking from the Panamint valley.
I don't wanna lose your love. I don't wanna lose your love. I don't wanna lose your love.

John Lennon: 'Beautiful Boy': Cottonwood mountain clouds. Silver gapes crack into thirst.
Close your eyes have no fear. The monster's gone, he's on the run and your daddy's here.

Pet Shop Boys: 'Always on my Mind'. Telegraph poles stitched into Centennial blackness.
Little things I should have said and done. I just never took the time. You were always on my mind.

Philip Oakey & Giorgio Moroder: 'Together in Electric Dreams'. Towne Pass Colossus. Sunlight rips the Butte in half.
We'll always be together, however hard it seems. We'll always be together, together in electric dreams.

Kate Bush, 'Running up that Hill' [……………………………………..]
Mute this. Get out the car. Breathe. Ignition.

Brand New Heavies: 'Get Back to Love'. A windscreen wasp blots Rainbow Canyon.
Time to discover why we're all feeling this way. Let's let love have its day.

Madonna: 'Into the Groove'. Six boulders on Mosaic Canyon freezeframe a family.
Only when I'm dancing do I feel this free. At night I lock the door where no-one else can see.

                                              Sidewinder:

                                    What issss your intention

                                                                    ???
                                                        ???

                                                                    ???

I
want
to
bury
some-
thing

              so
              the
              air

              can't touch you.

Take off your skin—

                quartz into silicon

                white globes surround

                the consent of oxygen

Take off your skin—

                blush of atomical redness

                so much molecular pressure

                to live inside a life

Take off your skin—

                grief's abacus of rain

                death's hand-me-downs

                cold certainty of the slab

Take off your skin—

                vanish in a reck of flesh

                into the exploding stillness

                this shattering of sound

6am slowfire. Heat steps along the Pinnacles,

a glower of sand at Trona, the valley's theatre

of dust evaporating over Panamint Springs

until Wildrose, where the dash locks on 100º.

Drive into Stovepipe Dunes with a medicine

bag flailing around the throat. What turns itself

on the hearing wheel of vastness gone quiet?

Stagecoach cactus basket outside the museum.

Estrangement as reticence. Metabolic, not quite.

As if I could find you without touch, like an idea

out of reach, yet reached for. As if being here

means the gallant outdoorsman, not your typical

tourist overlooker. Audition for the part of grief's

chameleon. Cut. The light still rises over your

shoulder. As if being here meant it were enough

to bear this absence without the absence of air.

Violence meaning

passage.

Timeblood.

Among things inadvertent
you left me, brother,

(leaving….

empty space,

…)

Under the rhyolite dome of Red Hill

    drumsmoke evaporates

        the kindness of a blue sky.

          .   .

                  Mirage horizon

                  (Real as pixels)

                  Past Funeral Mountain

                  (There is no pass)

                  Flush as laceration

                  (The dead as alive)

                      . . . . .

        To meet you here / I cannot

                              meet you.

        To sidewind the clock.

                       Unpunished

(unpunish)

  .

      To survive it

              (you could not survive it)

Enough antsypants. Enough conspiratorial psalmssss.

Wherever I move I spell

J

      your name
          in the sand...

J

      What are you
      prepared to
            sac
            rif
            ice

              ???

   ???

                ???

Wadjet.　　　　　Egyptian goddess of fertility. Pythons
　　　　　　　　　　　　　　curled over her ears.

Wadjet　　　　statue to pay back a loan from dad when your Camden business
　　　crashed.

WORLD ARTEFACTS

We drank the profits　　　　　　　　you stepping out of a rickshaw in Goa,
　　　your head pulled through
　　　　　　　　　　　the 'O' in a t-shirt
　　　　　　　　　　　　　　　　　spelling:

　　　　　　　　　　　　　　　　　　　　　　LOVE

　　　　What of this remains unpaid?　　　　　　　~~Death~~

　　　　What is a loan between father & son?

　　　　　　　　　　　　　　　　　　　　　　O. Oh.

Sparring with life—

Brotherly pontificate—you said, more than once—

Why don't you just settle down and have a child?

　　　　　　　　　Our Gaia on who you would beam
　　　　　　　　　　　　　　　　LOVE

　　　　　　　　　　　　　　　　, Rob,
　　　　　　　　　　　　　　　~~[this is not a signature]~~

Death sparring with life—

　　　　　　　Gaia,

conceived on inheriting the goddess.

40 pounds　　　　　priceless,
　the handwritten tag you inked on her neck—

　　　　　　　　　　Take it.　　　　　　　Just take it.

But there are no pythons in Death
Valley.

I should know. You
should know.

Could your mouth even
articulate the Shoshoni

for snake—

                                                do
                                 you
                                        kno
                              w
                                            wh
                            at issss
                            Shoshoni
                            for
                                       sn
                                       ake
                                       ???

`What issss snake?

        Call me tannakkaintsi /
        tannakkentsi but ssstill
        you don't kno
        w.

                Where issss your
        brother…
                    ???

[…………..]

In the parenthesis of fourteen months.

In memoriam.

        Power of possession to break apart me-
                              mory.

                Your deathroom,
                      the shattered bed
                              on which you died.

              We had to saw each ashy panel
                    in half

     just to get
              the sunken frame
                          out the door.

The 'O' in sound gone quiet. Time

to transpose your carcass of ambition

                                        gone/wrong.

The melancholy stigmata of goodbyes.

        Somethings we might share /

        / might have shared. But didn't.

                        (Revision sorrows   into
                                    past tense).

Every dimple
a grain of sand. Every harvest
                still
        burning.

Currency of paytime meaning
time to pay up

        Replay
              or repay.

Again………………….......

What are you to sacrifice

      ???

        Repay
              or replay

Again……………………..

What are you

      ???

<

bridge vertigo's / highways / overpasses

agoraphobia / anomie / unwalkable / un-

wakeable sound / the deedforge / in dying

the unbreak / broken / furnacing / in Bad

-water / the salt basin road / centuries-dry /

death as spitback / but nothing to drink / as

if you could / tie up the mule to its owners /

ghost / amid this / everywhere of violence

>

Inventory

- Four white sage smudge bulbs   burning and scrubbing
- Hollywood Walk of Fame stone plate   cracked
- Medicine bag   goatskin leather
- Rose quartz   love
- Tourmaline   healing
- Stone urn   letters burned to ash
- Blessing oil   Ceridwen's
- Ritual bowl   speckled
- Cloudwalking cream   insomnia
- Snake candle   sidewinder
- Zebra wood pen   Maturango
- Brass Kenyan wristband   tortoise
- Texts on sage and shamanism   no magicking back
- Oscar Wilde   postcard, unwritten
- Gold notebook   language too late
- Hotel tears   swabbed

Memory un-
memory.

       —striation of slitherous rock—

      —desert contras

      —the wishbone of language pulled

                        out of luck—

      [′′′   ′′′   ′′′   ′′′]

Smear the triglycerides in after a lukewarm shower.

Sleep as sacrifice. Coyote breath.

                You exit the dream with a totem fox

                        squatting the end of the bed.

Inventory

- Skull

    Día de los Muertos.
    Heartholes in the temple.

- 'Death Valley' t-shirt

    Abstract over literal,
    but fashionable (you
    would insist—

    When we cleared your room,
    we threw away bag after bag
    of ash-soaked designer
    clothes.

    Nothing you'd wear out).

- Water

    The dashboard needle
    measures 103º Fahrenheit.

- CBDs

    Painkiller silence.

- Sand

    Furnace glass echoing
    over Trona hills.

　　　　　　　　　Labyrinth you—

　　　　　　　　　　　　　　　interseen when camouflage

　　　　　　　　　　　　　　　omenic, to be unselved,

　　　　　　　　　　　　　　　hidden every day in public.

You came out two years after telling me

　　　　Keep everything a secret.

　　　Hardened in your case shell,

　　　　　　unready for bully's ruin.

　　Silence, once thrown to hedges,

　　　　　　living underground.

　　　　　　　　　　Among everyone who let you down

　　　　　　　　　　the most difficult relationship—

　　　　　　　　　　　　　　　self as yourself.

Foucault tripped out under feast stars to declare:

It was the greatest experience of my life.

A(ntionini) – Z(abriskie). Desire's endlessness

meets the solemn prospect(or) in his own portrait

(translation: Borax Inc. and the schist of propaganda).

Mess of orgiastic hair. Loose flakes of sand.

The desert as perpetual return. Returning.

How everything slips through the fingers or is

blown apart. Even the mind. In The End.

The dead as perpetual return. Unreturning.

Medicine bag like a lung

    sucking in wind on Dante's Peak.

                                              Hiss of the living.

                                           Redrock to salt basin.

                                                                 His /
                                                                 Hiss.

Dante dissolved into mesquite leaf—

                    …two figures mingled

                                          into one face,
          in which
                both were lost.

No. I will not give you

    Gaia's plaster of vaccination blood.

<Alphabet of Losses,
Artist's Palette>

A for Alison. Her brother gone yet conversant after a decade (Amber)
B who lost her father. Anything but 'dying' or 'death'. It is 'his passing' (Lime)
C who couldn't hold his mother's hand in the ambulance (Umber)
D who hit a 40 miles per hour sign doing 80 (Adriatic)
E who tried CPR before the second seizure. 'But why did you have to die?' (Abalone)
F fractalized by death. Who lives again after burying the sun (Fire Brick)
G for Gaia, your uncle gone and your umbilicus in a locked drawer (Tiger)
H in Jedda, winding up the memory box of loss (Maroon)
I grieving you. All the places we never went and went but never leave (Violet)
J whose parents died on the same day, apart but knowing (Cornflower)
K your mother and father in Derby, via Amritsar. 'Sorry' is never enough (Coffee)
L whose father's face kaleidoscopes in a bottle of single malt (Lava)
M for Mum. The laguna of burying your own son (Rose)
N still walking the penumbra streets of Dublin (Dust Brown)
O for Olga echoing in hallway mirrors (Ivory)
P nightshifting the emergency ward, masked to the eyes (Canyon)
Q who renamed himself the devil's psychic. Who is empty yet purulent (Ecru)
R for Tony: there's nothing that compares to the death of a sibling'. And he knew (Purple Satin)
S for you, Sidewinder. Hissing like a mine (Sapphire)
T for Toby, carving the wood of his mother's coffin (Chenna)
U in Amaranth Pink, singing 'Rebel, Rebel' through the kitchen.
V for Li Wenliang. The Wuhan Whistleblower (Bone)
W who staked everything on a blast of new cells (Dark Slate Grey)
X for K Za Win, who shielded children from a rain of bullets (Fulvous)
Y the Shoshoni, at the hands of the so-called 'pioneer' (Red Ochre)
Z your encore, your platinum laughter. Steel teal in a palette of loss.

To think of you at your lowest point

in the lowest point of the Western

hemisphere. Badwater: metabolise this.

Walk through salt. Wallblood. Sandhour.

Brother: nobody can harm you anymore.

Miocenic insignia. Glass inside clavicles

of rock. Quartz breath of oxygen. Agora-

phobia, the limping brother, heal with salt.

Unsuffer a life. No more counting cracks

in pavement slabs. Goodbye. A sudden release

of pressure. The city's gridded constrictions.

Be good to yourself and something good will

happen said the celebrant. Cloudshadow

unthreads Thorndike, drifts over Mahogany

Mountain like a form of breath released.

You, the child, the petrified angel, the adult

who always wanted to leave. Leave.

*<for Mulligan,
at Furnace Creek
Golf course>*

We aren't golfers. 'A good walk
spoiled' said Wilde, his face
winking out from my tote bag
(Oscar was Rob's favourite).

And anyway, in this furnace,
neither of us could carry a bag
of irons further than I sliced
into Aughton's duckpond.

$104°$, what's that in Celsius?
Putter really could melt
in your mouth out here,
even the cypress trees whistle

heat. And what 'rough' means
on the Devil's golf course
is snakebite (not the kind
you or I downed as kids).

Tee up on the 16th and fry.
Dogleg left, down the burning
fairway. Dante's *Inferno*,
the last ring of the bell.

The man in the Shoshoni office (Covid-closed) says:

        'Well, you're telling me you're a writer…

            but you could be from Nevada,

              or anywhere

                  like that'

Silence as vertebrae on Funeral Mountain

                      snaps.

           Sun   breaking

                 over loose shale—

death as silhouette

                 turned arid.

The place you go is always

            there
not
            here—

                              Dark holes in the sky

                              reconstruct a face.

All this   towards this

                                      disquiet of dust

                                                      to dust.

Two days…Two days

                before the coroner phoned to tell us you were dead.

Nobody to balm you.

                To hold your hand as you leaned out of life.

                [……………………………………….]

Skid into a dirt path   ~~dust to dust~~   ,

                echo encryption via Telescope Peak.

                Sometimes you are so close

                      it doubles just to shout your name—

                                ROBIN
                                ROBIN

            Desert: alluvial fossil   in the ashflow,

                    why this sudden

                                spectacle

                                      of rain?

                Wipe down my face

                                            my eyes.

<Badwater,
Shamanic initiation ritual
(Steps 1-4 (spoken) & 6th step:
automatic writing).

'Immediately within the opening or on the other side of the opening, make yourself see a dimly lit tunnel […] that descends downward either sharply or gently. The tunnel may be only a few feet long or it might seem as long as a city block, leading straight ahead or bending. When you are in sight of the tunnel's end, or you can see – or make yourself see – a brighter, well-lit area just beyond. That is the edge of the Otherworld.'

– T. Cowan

1. Lie on the floor on your back with a pillow beneath your knees. Place a bandana or scarf over your eyes to deepen the darkness behind your eyelids. Try to be as limp or relaxed as possible. Take a few deep breaths and see the location in nature where your entry is.

Tunnel entrance to an old grotto.

    Like St. John's at Patmos.

It is completely dark, just a patch of light from the entrance.

                                                        [……….]

    Is this the tunnel's end
                      or did I just come through this way?

[…………………..]

                        Brother, what is your revelation?

2. Look around this place of entry for a few moments as you previously practiced, engaging your senses, noticing colours, shapes, sights and sounds, then go through the entry and make yourself see the tunnel if it is not spontaneously there. Proceed down it toward the lighted area at the end.

    3. When you emerge in a landscape of some sort, look around. Call your power animal...

You looked at me
        from the flood marker
                in the carpark—

                        desert fox:
                        Celtic spirit-guide to the underworld...

    ...Call your power animal to join you and ask it to show you around this area just inside the Otherworld

take me inside where what is

unseen / is there / to be seen.

                                      <:::::**JOLT**:::::

                    Smoke courses through the ashpile.

                    Death's entrails ::::   tongue-torn :::::>

Why bring me to this
dank grotto, brother?

          You used to sleep with the light on,

     it's so dark in here.

                                        Where are you?

                                        Where are you?

Sage smudge left wrist.

Burning scent of cauterised   flesh

                                        <what is born
                                                                        breaks

                                        <Bits of brine
                                                                  and twig,

                                   sores
                                          of language.

                                                           Sage
                                          smoke
                        creeps from the walls.

                        A glacier of soda ash
                        distilled in your palm—

                                   glass into sand,

                        scatterwind

                                   beneath the gnarled
                                              tree

                        where you were
                                          born>.

Sage smudge right wrist

Desert made / unmade

                        of   breaking   glass.

4. Lie on the floor listening to a drumbeat. This part in your awareness will hear a change in drumming. At this point tell your power animal that it is time to return. Your power animal will take you back through the tunnel so you can emerge upward through the original opening. Spend a few moments reorienting yourself before you open your eyes.

        Tunnel meaning:

        way in / way out.

How slowly
        the moon passes

    over your eyes.
                           Wake up—

                                You
                         love
                                too
                       much
                         what
                     isss
                                   gone.

To leave, to arrive—
            what does it mean   in the afterskin,
                    at the collection
                          of your body?

                                     Sss
                                     ...
                              stay awhile

                No. Take me back.
                                  Nobody
                               comes
                                     back.

Desert fox: who looks away first?

                              Who possesses
                              who
                            ? ? ? ? ? ? ? ? ? ?
                Take me back.

                                     nonono

Brother,   you never asked to come here.

~~I never asked you to come here~~

~~I needed to know~~

        what to do / what to do?

    Salvia. Salvage.

You wait inside
a stoneboned old grotto.

    And I can't see you

in the buried darkness.

                      …His story…
                        …His hiss…

                      Who said the dead
                      are ever free
                      ? ? ? ? ? ? ? ? ? ?

        <Blood on sage

        a scarred moon>

      Your face refracts
      inside the glass.

          You are the tunnel,
          the entrance and exit.

                      ? ? ? ? ? ? ? ? ? ?
                      ? ? ? ? ? ? ? ? ? ?

              Let me out.

Trona sand /
Badwater salt

Rub the grains
into your bare hands.

The mule stoops
into a smile.

                      Desert fox.
                      Rose quartz.
                      Tourmaline.
                      Sagebrush.

                      Desert fox.
                      Rose quartz.
                      Tourmaline.
                      Sagebrush.

                      Desert fox.
                      Rose quartz.
                      Tourmaline.
                      Sagebrush.

                      […………..]

                                          Ashbreath in the ritual bowl.

                                                        Time to go.

<Sixth step>

Radiant the boy buying daffodils for his mum
the greengrocer must have said to the florist
when you walked in seven years old on Mother's
Day too small to count out your change
on the counter. mountain see this. fill me
with smoke's forgiveness. you died in your bed
thinking you were having a panic attack last thing
before sleep. you died on your bed and Damian
didn't even call the ambulance or police or
fuckhead even tell us you had died. the mortuary
called the numbers you left beside the bed.
we go where in the sand when we cannot say
goodbye. you were 46. 46. pour the blessing
oil. sagebrush burn through this missing you.
salt as residue from the lowest point on earth.
let me live with you / without you. salvia.
heal. Learning to hear you quiet. The sound
of breaking glass unmemoried but not
gone. always knowing both you and me

<Furnace Creek>

Black tomentum, sing
the rabbit, the thrasher,
the sparrow's mania.
Sing of the Naqual.
The waking artist.

*

Black totem, fire-
chambered, in the hand,
wristlet wave to anklet.
Dance through smoke
towards another flame.

*

Black tomentum, sing
Salvia apiana salvare,
heal grief's poultice
that is thinking: I could
have taken you in, brother.

					Two full moons
					hung over you
					last night:

				which did you ssssee
				? ? ? ? ? ? ? ? ? ? ? ? ?

					One stretched out
				like a blur of lightning.
				Radiating with the dead.

					The other was quieter,
				venomous as the living.

				Which one did you ssssee
				? ? ? ? ? ? ? ? ? ? ? ? ?

						Inside one of these,

								I live.

The Republicans—Bill and Candy—
enter the pool with their teenage son
trailing a few yards behind and the gate
slams everyone awake. 'Bill Jr. C'mon
over here!' and they slap down towels
while Candy—in stars n' stripes bikini—
bellyflops in, spraying the eastern deck,
and crashing a few strokes of butterfly,
as if she were the conductor of a giant
wave machine. Bill Jr. pokes his earbuds
in delicately as if composting them,
while mum returns a length talking loud—
that G.I. show last year in Nevada.
'Hell yeah. We should go again'
says Bill Snr. stroking his crotch.
And so on and so much that I
have to dive in and blubblubblub
stick my head under the water.
'How the price of guns went up
crazy in Pahrump'. 'Harrumph'
replies the teenager and they laugh—
Snr. first, as if giving permission,
for the son to join in. Hahahaha.
Blubblubblub. Voices wettened
down, blur into goggle fog.

The Shoshoni elder smiles:

'Okay, you can have two words…

                          …you want me to tell them to you?

Our language is sacred,

            why would we share it

                      with just

                                    anyone?'

At the bar, three American jocks foghorn over a round of shots:

      'And anyway, 'anyway' should be one word, asshole'

    'I have so many transactions it's into the thousands'

      'My whole life story is written in receipts'

                                      'Boulder here we come!'

< film script
plus visual text:
Zabriskie Point,
0-1hr 15mins>

the problem as translating that
bullshit jazz
there's a lot of […]
white people
what's going to make white people
turn into revolutionaries
getting what they deserve
the enemy is visible
we do not have white support
when the cops move in
on the strike lines
strategically
black people earned this leadership
in blood
he's okay
even anarchists spend most of their lives
in meetings

what book?
why don't you just eat in the cafeteria?
who will give me permission?
a book? I just work when I need bread
Heller Machinery. Rentals. Benedict. Alice
my sister be prepared
is that your slogan? Serious,
it's not a game
some of these people over here need
medical attention
you didn't say you were a doctor
you thought the rules didn't apply to you
keep your hands up

name?
Karl Marx.
how do you spell it?
M A R X
we need some guns right away
but the law was made for peacetime
i wouldn't recommend anything
smaller than a '38

G
U
N
S

take your son out
quail hunting in the wide open spaces
like pioneers who moulded the west
sunny dunes
house in the sun
need a job?
the time has come
development
investment
carrying a packet of seeds

yeh I mind
goodbye hello
liberal art
mortuaries
you want extra
you pay extra
if I trust in you I'd have to
trust everyone in the whole world
Lilly 7
the cost of blasting
rock slopes
you think of things

not now stupid
Frostie
rumpus room
god damn it

hey listen
hey come back
hey kid where's jimmy?
thanks for the nightie but I don't think
I can use it
I needed to get off the ground
extracurricular activities
haha
stop it

once I changed my colour but it didn't work
it's getting like they don't even report it
unless 300 are killed
just like old john brown

hey whatever your name is
hey toughguy, are you alright?
don't you feel at home here?

let's play a deathgame
and the winner will get to play the loser

like a happy childhood
a dead pioneer
whooooowoooh
uuurmmmmmm
hey hey

so anyway river
it 'aint table salt

Antonioni fucking in the mule pass.

        Wrapped in sunset's loincloth.

                All that wrestling of privilege.

The boy gets the girl

        then implodes.

                Doesn't think of her.

                …Thinking of you…

                …Wish you were…

    : in the dust with your Mark (who died a decade before) :

      Up close,

           it's all a tangle of the living and the dead.

Eat up. The chicken arrives
    drawn and quartered.

        STALL CLOSED

        SOCIAL DISTANCING

        IN EFFEC

        TOILET PROB.

Wake up. Wake up   the one who is awake.

Thank you, that was a lovely meal.

    The waiter's smile
        inside my head
            transluces:

        Go to Ballarat. Meet my aunt
        Queenie Rose.

        The dead wait
            like glass inside sand.

        Go to Ballarat. Ghost town.

        The dead wait
            like time made of blood.

Lumix precarious
over the cliff's edge.

       Click.
              Click.
       Click.

'Nice to meet you…Patsy, did you say?'

'Sorry, Patsy, I don't know from here where the moon rises.'

              [.......]

              'Oh', then you're here for the sun.'

'No, I'm here to bury a sound.'

              [.......]

              'Oh, *Ooooo*'.

    She moves away to her husband,

              'Richard, Richie darling'.

    Surveyor eyes scan Twenty Mule canyon
        like a Borax prospector hovering
           over a green flame.

Viewfinder entrance of a young girl

        (a ringer for Daria Halprin
        from the casting couch of the street).

She wants ice cream.

        'Where's the Ben n' Jerry's round here,
    anyway—

        I'm tired of all this desert.
            Let's just go home.'

                                                                    <Ballarat,
                                                                 Ghost Village>

A dirt path levels out to ask:
                             what survives?

The owner's phantom double drives out as you enter—

            his wave friendly,

            his smile mocking,
                                                        As if you could
                                                         passss Charon.

Through smashed hinges of a doorway

            the trading post sign declares itself

                                                OPEN

but a skeleton playing harpsichord says

                                                CLOSED

Skeleton:	did you come this way?

        Only the dead come this way.

                Where are you?

                        I am here.

                    Where are you?

                              Where are you?

BloodBrother.

        Walls that locked you in.

                Fall a decade, a century.

          Dis/place. Ghost town revisiting

          the site of our collective
                            demise.

          As if death could play out the living

          As if to speak to you. Eyes closed.

                                             art-
                                               i
                                           - fice
                                               !

                          This morning your brother
                                          and i
                                       ate schist
                                   for breakfast.

                           Walk up the thorn pass
                                 to the stanchion.
                              I'll be waiting there
                            dressed as lumber.

A razor cuts the hand—

Tump the seal down with sand
        and a thumb of blood.

                                          Enter the door
                                            of the old
                                                ~~morgue~~
                                              jailhouse,
                                          the fire hiss
                                            of my tongue.

—————————————nonononono——————————————

Everything sealed
                      release.

The sun's severed eye pours

        through an urn of sand

The blue sky flattens into dust.

                              Wipe the blood

                              from my hands,

                                    your feet—

You are free,

                brother,

                                          you are free.

<Zabriskie Point coda,
final scene>

To ex/plode. To survive beyond fridges and flying chickens. Weight of mirrors. Of libraries. The screaming glass of television. Rename it distillation. Splintering of the cacti. Your eyes must have wanted to protect me across the lounge room. Perhaps I only remember the hideous carpet. The lightning terror of my pulse. Maybe I was looking away. Looking down at the miracle of my newborn hand. Detonate the not-know. Ex/plode glass back into sand. Plosive flints on the road home. Just let the bully's try and find you now. Shriek quieter than an under-radar. Unheard even when the drums fingle in. Sound shaken back into shock comets. Beyond cobblestones of voice. The intimacy of shoes. Taken off. Taken out. Graspable yet invisible. What it is to live with you as air. Simple as breathing or screaming in the asphyxiation of dust. Can you see me through the daily mask. Smiling at you like water brisked by wind. What remains is the red cloth of grief. Still. The important things are never washed clean. Language names some/thing. Try writing the word 'glass' with a stick of fire. Detonation unkeeping you for company. Let the living wardrobe you carried on your back. Loosen into kindling. A sound of glass passes the eye like tears of laughter. The pantry beserks. On the way down I'll catch you. I'm sorry, so sorry. On the way out. I was miles off. As if one day it will be as easy as getting back into the car and simply driving away. No. Silence in the song keeps playing through. Hear it to live with it. To converse you dead. To be comfortable with the screech in my skin. Sunlight dims a valley's concave horizon. Makes it sound easy as watching clouds migrate somewhere new. Close the door. Open the door. Childhood blue sky. Everyday threats. Hear those voices now you'll have a reply. Ex/plosion. Fire into air. Light it up. Not dressing as a wound. You're in charge now. Nobody good enough to give you a start writes the last scene. Fire the dark. Burn the rafters. Every window breaks open and walks through you. There's a hammer in your foot. Why shouldn't things be different now. No more blood left to give. The presenter on the screen disappears into sand. Nobody scoping you out on the street. Nothing left of fear. The onion world will skin itself. Tears in the urn. What was broken that was once you. Transmutes. Quartz into silica. The sound of glass (un)shattering. In The End. It hurts and never goes away. With us, but not. With us. It is always you.

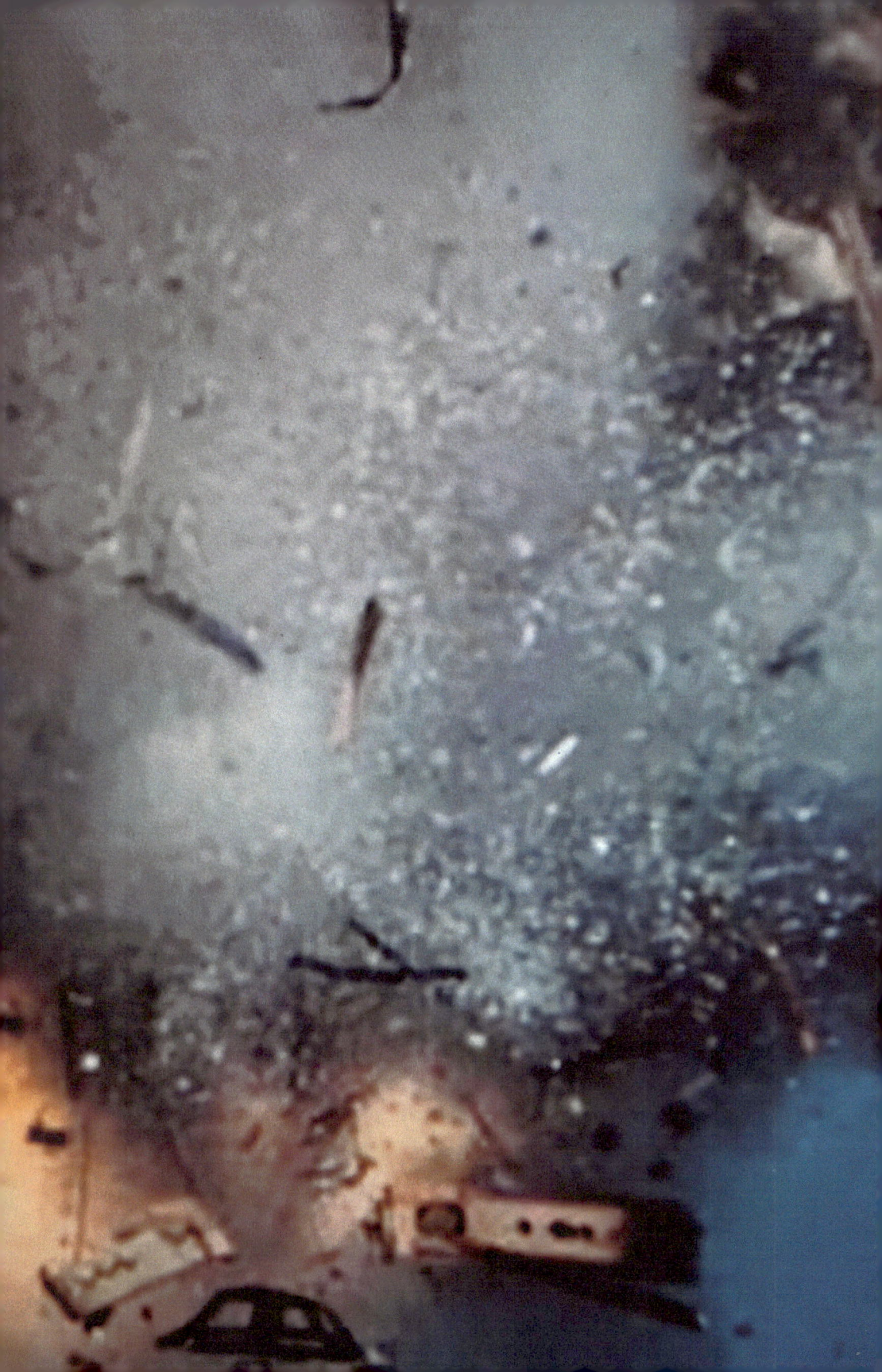

Notes / Acknowledgements

Epigraph quotes: 'A Robin Red breast in a Cage' is from William Blake's 'Auguries of Innocence' (Pickering Manuscript, 1803, first published 1863). 'Look closer–his skin is a desert' is from Natalie Diaz's collection *When my Brother was an Aztec* (Copper Canyon, 2012). 'the closer threat of life behind the glass' from Jayanta Mahapatra's poem 'Glass' (published in *Poetry*, July 1976). '…la llaga melancólica de los adioses.'. 'The melancholy stigmata of goodbyes' is from Jaime Saenz's *Immanent Visitor: Selected Poems of Jaime Saenz*, translated by Kent Johnson and Forrest Gander (University of California Press, 2002)

The jukebox section includes quotes from the following artists and tracks: Primal Scream, 'Loaded', single from the album *Screamadelica*, Creation Records (1991); John Lennon: 'Beautiful Boy (Darling Boy)', single from the album *Double Fantasy,* Geffen Records (1980)' Pet Shop Boys: 'Always on my Mind', single from the album *Introspection*, Parlophone (1988); Philip Oakey & Giorgio Moroder: 'Together in Electric Dreams', from the soundtrack album *Electric Dreams*, Virgin Records (1984); Brand New Heavies: 'Get Back to Love', single from the album *Brother Sister*, Delicious Vinyl (1994); Madonna: 'Into the Groove', single from the album *Like a Virgin*, Sire Records (1984)

Shoshoni words for 'snake' were found on the archive: https://shoshoniproject.utah.edu/language-materials/shoshoni-dictionary/dictionary.php?filter=T

The translation from Dante's *Inferno* was made by the author.

'…the limping brother' bears reference to Paul Carter's *Repressed Spaces: The Poetics of Agoraphobia*, Reaktion Books (2002).

All quotes from T. Cowan during the Badwater ritual are taken from *Shamanism as spiritual practice for daily life*, Crossing Press (1996).

"Ghost town revisiting / the site of our collective // demise." is a riff on Dr Katy Layton Jones' commentary in 'Why we are so fascinated with ghost towns?', a collaborative piece between the BBC and Open University: https://www.bbc.co.uk/ideas/videos/why-are-we-so-fascinated-by-ghost-towns/p09qkxpw

Michelangelo Antionini's *Zabriskie Point* (1970) is referred to a various points in this text. The write through of the text on page 84 includes passages of script dialogue but also advertising hoardings and any texts visible in the film.

The still on page 85 is an image of the film's final scene, which is written through in the preceding 'coda'.

All photographs in this book (except the cover photograph) are from the author's personal archive and are not to be reproduced without permission. They were shot using a Lumix GH5.

*   *   *   *

This book is dedicated to my brother, but is also for our parents and siblings.

I would also like to acknowledge Ashwini Bhat and Forrest Gander for giving me a moment to think these notes out. Thanks also to Fred D'Aguiar, sj fowler and the three Chris's (Madden, McCabe, Routledge). In solidarity with Julie Goldsmith, Toby Mercer, Nieves Garcia Prados, Tony Ward, Alison Trower. With special thanks to Aaron Kent and all at Broken Sleep Books.

Always, to Sandeep and now to Gaia, who is life.

Robin, dear brother. Be at peace.

LAY OUT YOUR UNREST

www.ingramcontent.com/pod-product-compliance
Lightning Source LLC
Chambersburg PA
CBHW042326150426
43192CB00004B/124